Paul Revere's Ride

THE LANDLORD'S TALE

By Henry Wadsworth Longfellow

Illustrated by Charles Santore

HARPERCOLLINSPUBLISHERS

For his assistance, I'd like to thank Mr. Herb Jacobs—C.S.

Paul Revere's Ride: The Landlord's Tale / Illustrations copyright © 2003 by Charles Santore
Manufactured in China. All rights reserved. / www.harperchildrens.com

Library of Congress Cataloging-in-Publication Data
Longfellow, Henry Wadsworth, 1807–1882.
 Paul Revere's ride: the landlord's tale / by Henry Wadsworth Longfellow ; illustrated by Charles
Santore.
  p. cm.
 ISBN 0-688-16552-4 — ISBN 0-06-623747-5 (lib. bdg.)
 1. Revere, Paul, 1735–1818—Juvenile poetry. 2. Lexington, Battle of, 1775—Juvenile poetry.
3. Children's poetry, American. [1. Revere, Paul, 1735–1818—Poetry. 2. Lexington, Battle of,
1775—Poetry. 3. American poetry. 4. Narrative poetry.] I. Santore, Charles, ill. II. Title.
PS2271.P3 2003   00-039704
811'.3—dc21   CIP
                                                                                          AC

Typography by Al Cetta   1 2 3 4 5 6 7 8 9 10   ❖   First Edition

To Eugene Pettinelli, my friend, who has been there
for me from the beginning
—C.S.

Listen, my children, and you shall hear
Of the midnight ride of Paul Revere,
On the eighteenth of April, in Seventy-five;
Hardly a man is now alive
Who remembers that famous day and year.

He said to his friend, "If the British march
By land or sea from the town to-night,
Hang a lantern aloft in the belfry arch
Of the North Church tower as a signal light,—
One if by land, and two, if by sea;
And I on the opposite shore will be,
Ready to ride and spread the alarm
Through every Middlesex village and farm,
For the country folk to be up and to arm."

Then he said, "Good-night!" and with muffled oar
Silently rowed to the Charlestown shore,
Just as the moon rose over the bay,
Where swinging wide at her moorings lay
The Somerset, British man-of-war;
A phantom ship, with each mast and spar
Across the moon like a prison bar,
And a huge black hulk, that was magnified
By its own reflection in the tide.

Meanwhile, his friend, through alley and street,
Wanders and watches with eager ears,
Till in the silence around him he hears
The muster of men at the barrack door,
The sound of arms, and the tramp of feet,
And the measured tread of the grenadiers,
Marching down to their boats on the shore.

Then he climbed the tower of the Old North Church,

By the wooden stairs, with stealthy tread,

To the belfry-chamber overhead,

And startled the pigeons from their perch

On the sombre rafters, that round him made

Masses and moving shapes of shade,—

By the trembling ladder, steep and tall,

To the highest window in the wall,

Where he paused to listen and look down

A moment on the roofs of the town,

And the moonlight flowing over all.

Beneath, in the churchyard, lay the dead,
In their night-encampment on the hill,
Wrapped in silence so deep and still
That he could hear, like a sentinel's tread,
The watchful night-wind, as it went
Creeping along from tent to tent,
And seeming to whisper, "All is well!"
A moment only he feels the spell
Of the place and the hour, and the secret dread
Of the lonely belfry and the dead;
For suddenly all his thoughts are bent
On a shadowy something far away,
Where the river widens to meet the bay,—
A line of black that bends and floats
On the rising tide, like a bridge of boats.

Meanwhile, impatient to mount and ride,
Booted and spurred, with a heavy stride
On the opposite shore walked Paul Revere.
Now he patted his horse's side,
Now gazed at the landscape far and near,
Then, impetuous, stamped the earth,
And turned and tightened his saddle-girth;
But mostly he watched with eager search
The belfry-tower of the Old North Church,
As it rose above the graves on the hill,
Lonely and spectral and sombre and still.

And lo! as he looks, on the belfry's height
A glimmer, and then a gleam of light!
He springs to the saddle, the bridle he turns,
But lingers and gazes, till full on his sight
A second lamp in the belfry burns!

A hurry of hoofs in a village street,

A shape in the moonlight, a bulk in the dark,

And beneath, from the pebbles, in passing, a spark

Struck out by a steed flying fearless and fleet;

That was all! And yet, through the gloom and the light,

The fate of a nation was riding that night;

And the spark struck out by that steed, in his flight,

Kindled the land into flame with its heat.

He has left the village and mounted the steep,
And beneath him, tranquil and broad and deep,
Is the Mystic, meeting the ocean tides;
And under the alders that skirt its edge,
Now soft on the sand, now loud on the ledge,
Is heard the tramp of his steed as he rides.

It was twelve by the village clock,
When he crossed the bridge into Medford town.
He heard the crowing of the cock,
And the barking of the farmer's dog,
And felt the damp of the river fog,
That rises after the sun goes down.

It was one by the village clock,

When he galloped into Lexington.

He saw the gilded weathercock

Swim in the moonlight as he passed,

And the meeting-house windows, blank and bare,

Gaze at him with a spectral glare,

As if they already stood aghast

At the bloody work they would look upon.

It was two by the village clock,
When he came to the bridge in Concord town.
He heard the bleating of the flock,
And the twitter of birds among the trees,
And felt the breath of the morning breeze
Blowing over the meadows brown.
And one was safe and asleep in his bed
Who at the bridge would be first to fall,
Who that day would be lying dead,
Pierced by a British musket-ball.

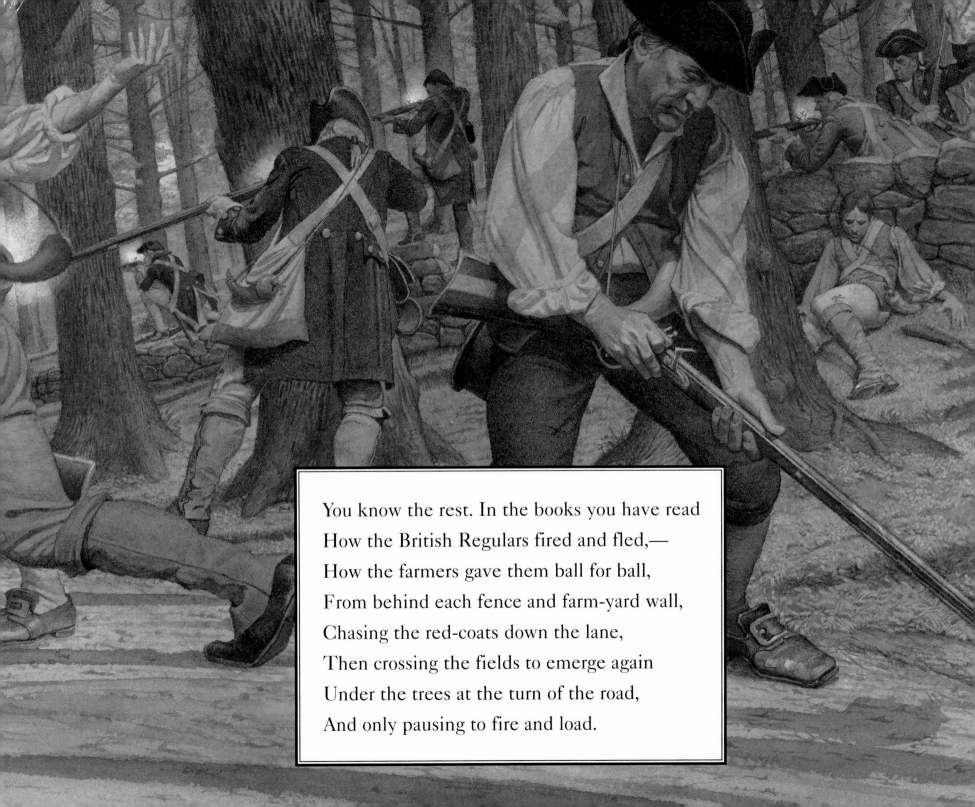

You know the rest. In the books you have read
How the British Regulars fired and fled,—
How the farmers gave them ball for ball,
From behind each fence and farm-yard wall,
Chasing the red-coats down the lane,
Then crossing the fields to emerge again
Under the trees at the turn of the road,
And only pausing to fire and load.

So through the night rode Paul Revere;

And so through the night went his cry of alarm

To every Middlesex village and farm,—

A cry of defiance, and not of fear,

A voice in the darkness, a knock at the door,

And a word that shall echo forevermore!

For, borne on the night-wind of the Past,

Through all our history, to the last,

In the hour of darkness and peril and need,

The people will waken and listen to hear

The hurrying hoof-beats of that steed,

And the midnight message of Paul Revere.

ARTIST'S NOTE

When editor Susan Pearson called to ask if I would be interested in illustrating Henry Wadsworth Longfellow's classic poem "Paul Revere's Ride," I was delighted. Like most American children of my generation, I had to read and recite the poem often in school, and I loved its stirring words. But how to begin the illustrations?

Fate was on my side. No sooner had I said "Yes" than I discovered *The Poetical Works of Henry Wadsworth Longfellow* on a bookshelf not two feet from my drawing board. It was a large, tattered, leather-bound volume published in Boston in 1879. The book had been a birthday gift from my daughter Christina, and I had not opened it in years. Immediately I searched the dusty volume for the poem and found that "Paul Revere's Ride" was part of a collection of poems titled "Tales of the Wayside Inn." After reading the collection, I could see that the Wayside Inn was a retreat dear to the poet's heart. The opening poem describes an evening by the fireside at the Inn where a group of friends are telling stories. Each in turn relates a tale. The first man to speak is the landlord, "a man of ancient pedigree," and this tale is "Paul Revere's Ride." The setting struck just the right note. There, by a blazing fire in the 1860s, the tale of an adventure that took place nearly one hundred years before unfolds. I knew then how my version of the poem would begin.

I proceeded to gather research from my files on Colonial costumes, locations, architecture, and the Revolutionary War. As I was going through a file on eighteenth-century American furniture, I found, much to my surprise, a letter from the Wayside Inn! Needless to say, I was very excited. Could this indeed be the Wayside Inn of the poem? Longfellow's Wayside Inn? I had no idea that the Inn was even still in existence.

The letter, which was about an eighteenth-century Windsor chair, had been sent to me in 1994 by Mr. Guy LeBlanc of the History and Preservation Department of Longfellow's Wayside Inn in Sudbury, Massachusetts. Now, five years later, finding the letter was quite astonishing, especially since my current focus was on "Paul Revere's Ride" and had nothing to do with Windsor chairs! I immediately called Mr. LeBlanc. I explained my project and my concept for the opening illustration—the landlord telling his tale to his friends by the fireside of the Wayside Inn. Mr. LeBlanc's response was more than generous. He not only confirmed that it was the same inn, but he also sent me photographs of the Parlor Museum room, the actual room where the friends gathered to tell their tales. And he included detailed photographs of the landlord's coat of arms, the mantelpiece, and the fireplace, as these were all specifically mentioned in Longfellow's poem.

All these details have made their way into my paintings, along with many other historical details about Colonial architecture, clothing, and even landscapes. I have loved my journey back to America's past, and I hope Mr. Longfellow— and the landlord—would be pleased.

Charles Santore

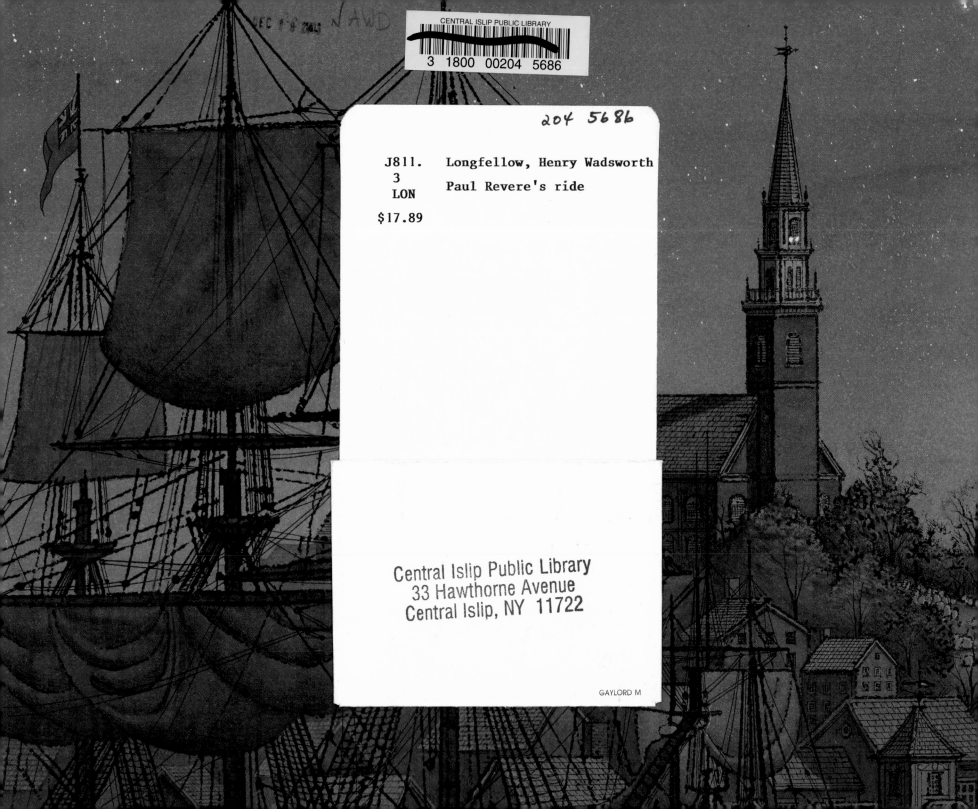